McD

Garter Snakes

by Mary Ann McDonald

Illustrated with photographs
by Joe McDonald

Capstone Press

MINNEAPOLIS

Printed in the United States of America.

Capstone Press • 2440 Fernbrook Lane • Minneapolis, MN 55447

Editorial Director   John Coughlan
Managing Editor   Tom Streissguth
Production Editor   Jim Stapleton
Book Designer   Timothy Halldin

Library of Congress Cataloging-in-Publication Data
McDonald, Mary Ann.
   Garter snakes / by Mary Ann and Joe McDonald;
   illustrated with photographs by the authors.
         p. cm.
   Includes bibliographical references (p. 46) and index.
   Summary: Describes the physical characteristics, habitat, and behavior of the common garter snake.
   ISBN 1-56065-295-0
   1. Garter snakes--Juvenile literature. [1. Garter snakes. 2. Snakes.] I. McDonald, Joe. II. Title
   QL666.O636M39 1996
   597.96--dc20   95-437
                                                          CIP
                                                          AC
00 99 98 97   8 7 6 5 4 3 2

Table of Contents

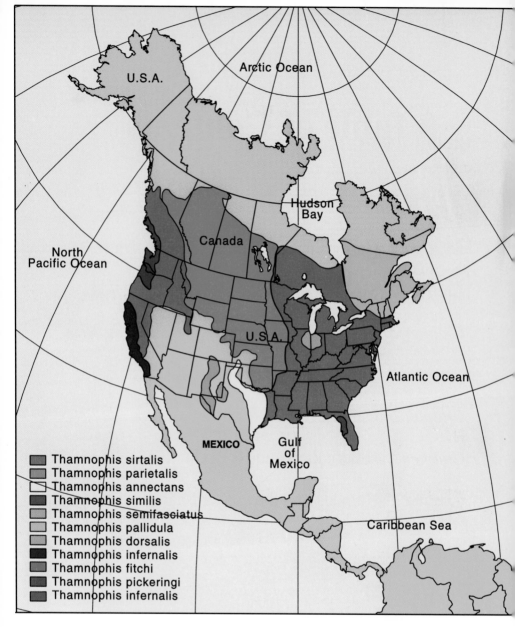

Thamnophis sirtalis
Thamnophis parietalis
Thamnophis annectans
Thamnophis similis
Thamnophis semifasciatus
Thamnophis pallidula
Thamnophis dorsalis
Thamnophis infernalis
Thamnophis fitchi
Thamnophis pickeringi
Thamnophis infernalis

There are 11 species of garter snakes living in the United States and Canada. The scientific name of each species begins with *Thamnophis*.

Facts about Garter Snakes

Scientific names: The scientific names for garter snakes begins with the name *Thamnophis*. Ribbon snakes also belong to this group of snakes.

Description: Garter and ribbon snakes are slim, round snakes ranging in length from 14 to 52 inches (35 to 132 centimeters). Most species have a yellowish back stripe and two side stripes running the length of their body.

Distinctive habits: Garter snakes hibernate, or sleep, during the colder months of the year.

Food: Garter and ribbon snakes eat frogs, toads, salamanders, and small fish.

Reproduction: Garter and ribbon snakes mate in the spring. The female gives birth to live young in the late summer or early fall. In some species, up to 85 young are born at one time.

Life span: As long as 10 years.

Habitat: Garter snakes live in mountains, prairies, meadows, coastal marshes, and even in cities.

Chapter 1

Garter Snakes

The garter snake is the most common snake in North America. It lives almost as far north as the Arctic Circle, in the Northwest Territories of Canada. Garters also live in many places in the United States and in northern Mexico.

You can find garters in many different habitats, including saltwater marshes near the sea and canyons high in the mountains. The western terrestrial garter snake can live at an elevation of 10,500 feet (3,200 meters). The

The eastern garter snake, or *Thamnophis s. sirtalis*, is a common species.

only place you won't find a garter snake is in a very hot desert.

Garter snakes are named for the garters that men wore many years ago. These were small elastic bands that held up socks. Many garters had stripes. People thought their striped garters looked a little like the striped snakes that sometimes appeared in their backyards.

Where They Live

Garter snakes adapt very easily to many surroundings, but they are most at home near water. They live and hunt in ditches, marshes, streams, lakes, and ponds. They eat frogs and salamanders but will also eat small mice and earthworms.

The ribbon snake is a type of garter that is always found in wet areas. Ribbon snakes eat only frogs, salamanders, tadpoles, and small fish. They bask, or lie, in the sun along shorelines. When frightened, they slip into the water and swim away.

A Snake in Danger

Despite the great number of garter snakes in North America, one variety is in trouble. The San Francisco garter snake is an endangered species. This snake is losing its habitat because of city development. Scientists are trying to save it by protecting certain wild areas. If they don't succeed, this snake will become extinct, and disappear from the wild.

The endangered San Francisco garter snake lives on the west coast of the United States.

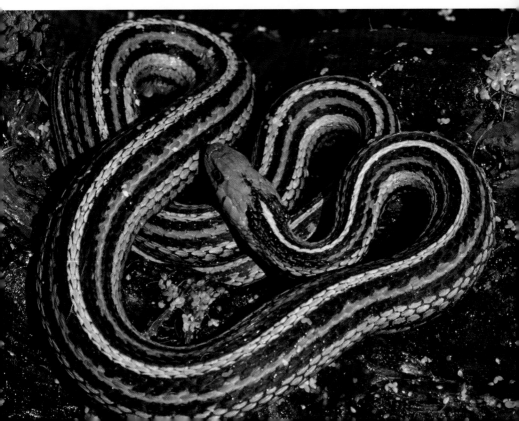

Chapter 2
Size and Color

Common garter snakes are the largest species in the genus (group) Thamnophis. They can reach lengths of 52 inches (132 centimeters) and can live as long as 10 years. Despite their size, garter snakes are rarely seen. They prefer to hide under rocks or logs. The best chance of seeing garters is in the spring, when they sit in the sun on rocks, logs, or bushes.

Camouflage allows this western aquatic garter snake to hide from its enemies.

A Snake of Many Colors

Garter snakes come in a wide range of colors, including brown, tan, olive, or black. Many have either yellow or orange stripes running down their backs and sides. Some have black patches on their sides, and some garters have no markings at all.

Some garter snakes have unusual color mutations—differences in their normal

Albino snakes have no color pigment in their skin.

coloring. Around Lake Erie and in parts of Nova Scotia, some garters are all black. Black absorbs heat better and helps the snakes to warm up faster while lying in the sun.

Some **albino** garter snakes exist in captivity. Albino animals have no color in their skin or eyes. Their eyes appear red, and their skin is either white or a light cream color. In the wild, albino snakes don't live very long. Predators would spot them and quickly eat them.

13

Scales and Brilles

Like all snakes, garters are covered with scales. These scales have ridges, or **keels**, running down their middles. The keels may help the snake to move.

The scales on a garter snake's head are large and smooth. They look polished. One thin scale

covers the snake's eyes. These thin, transparent scales are called **spectacles**, or **brilles**.

Shedding Skin

A snake grows throughout its entire lifetime. As it grows, it sheds its skin in a process called **ecdysis**. Before it sheds, the snake releases an oil underneath the outer layer of skin. This will separate the old skin from the new. The oil clouds the snake's eyes and makes them look blue. The snake's eyes clear up again just before shedding takes place.

To remove its old skin, the snake first rubs its head against something rough. After the skin tears open, the snake hooks it on a rock or branch. The snake then crawls out of its old skin, which is an exact copy of the new skin. If you look at an old snake skin, you can even see the eye scales.

Chapter 3

Movement

Garter snakes can move over many different surfaces. They can climb a bush, crawl under a log, swim on the surface of a pond, or glide through the grass. But they need a rough surface to help them move. If you put a garter snake on a smooth floor, it won't be able to crawl very well.

Tree bark provides a rough and useful surface for serpentine movement.

Garter snakes use serpentine motion over rough surfaces as well as through water and marsh.

Serpentine Motion

Garter snakes use several different types of motion. The most common type is called **serpentine motion**. The snake pushes its body from side to side to find rough surfaces. It then pushes itself off of these rough spots. Whatever path the head takes, the body and tail follow right behind. Garters use this motion to swim, too. From above, a swimming garter snake looks like it's just wiggling forward.

Concertina Motion

Sometimes, a garter snake moves in **concertina motion**. It uses this method in slippery or narrow areas. The snake anchors its tail and reaches forward with the upper part of its body. When it finds a rough spot, it holds on and pulls its tail forward. The process is repeated over and over again. This looks a little like the motion of a concertina, a kind of accordion.

Caterpillar Motion

To move in a straight line, the garter snake crawls in **caterpillar motion.** Using its large belly scales, called **scutes**, the snake digs into the ground. As it tightens and relaxes its muscles, the scutes pull the snake forward.

Garter snakes use different motions at different times. Larger snakes use the caterpillar motion most often. Serpentine motion is best for swimming. When a garter snake is in danger, it will use whatever motion is quickest in the surroundings.

It is rare to find a garter snake high in a tree. They sometimes sun themselves on low bushes. If trouble occurs, they quickly drop to the ground and hide. Garter snakes have many enemies. They must stay alert at all times, or they will become a meal for another animal.

Staying On Time

Many garter snakes have regular schedules. A garter may visit the same spot at the same time, day after day. To get warm after a cold night, a garter may bask in the sun during the morning hours. Later it may forage, or search for food, for a couple of hours. It will spend the rest of the day hiding from predators.

If you find a garter snake lying in the sun, check the time. The next day, check again at the same time. Write down whether it is sunny or cloudy. Keep observing the snake for about a week. Soon you'll know the snake's daily routine. By keeping records, you are becoming a **herpetologist**—a scientist who studies snakes and other reptiles.

Logs make good hiding places for the garter snake, which has many natural enemies.

Chapter 4

The Senses

Garter and ribbon snakes are **diurnal**, meaning they are active during the day. They are constantly searching along pond edges or under fallen logs for food. They must always stay alert and watch for danger, too.

Snake Eyes

Garter snakes are nearsighted and can't clearly see objects that are over 15 inches (38 centimeters) away. But they can see movement. This is very important when searching for prey. A garter might crawl right by a motionless frog, but it will chase after one that moves or jumps away.

Chapter 5

Defense

Garter and ribbon snakes have many different enemies. Birds, frogs, turtles, and other snakes eat baby snakes, which look like earthworms.

Larger snakes also have to watch for birds, like herons, egrets, and gulls. Hungry hawks and owls sit in trees waiting for a snake to crawl by. A robin once tried to eat a 20-inch (51-centimeter) garter snake. The snake was too large, and the robin choked to death as it tried to swallow its huge meal.

A red-shouldered hawk prepares to carry off a meal of fresh garter snake.

A young snake's camouflage didn't fool this hungry screech owl.

Mammals eat garter snakes, too. Raccoons, weasels, foxes, minks, and even bobcats often catch and eat snakes.

Snake Self-Defense

A garter snake has several ways to defend itself. If it can, the snake tries to crawl under something and hide. Sometimes a garter will slither a few feet and suddenly stop. The snake's colors help it to lie camouflaged, or disguised, among the leaves. It survives by lying still.

If the snake cannot hide itself, it may try to bite the attacker. First, the snake flattens itself and spreads the muscles in its head. This makes it look larger and more dangerous. Then it may strike. The garter snake has a small mouth and small teeth. Its bite usually won't hurt its enemy. But it may give the snake enough time to escape.

Messy Musk

If all else fails, the garter snake gives off a slimy, greasy **musk** from underneath its tail. This musk has a bad smell, and it probably doesn't taste very good, either. Attackers will spit a smelly snake out of their jaws. With the bad smell and taste, the attacker may think the snake is dead and leave it alone.

If you try to pick up a wild garter snake, you will probably be slimed with this musk. It will stick to your hands and to your clothes, and it will smell for a long time. Pet snakes lose their fear and rarely use this weapon.

Lynxes are quick enough to catch garter snakes. But they are always careful to avoid getting slimed.

A ribbon snake prepares to swallow a big meal.

Hunting

Garter and ribbon snakes must eat constantly to stay alive. Both types of snakes are carnivorous, meaning they will eat meat. What the snake eats depends on its size. Its prey ranges in size from slugs to small mice.

Garter snakes do not have a poisonous bite. Without venom, or poison, to help kill their prey, they have to just grab their food and start eating. A garter snake wouldn't be able to catch a large animal. The animal would escape as soon as the snake moved its jaws to start eating.

Garters, like other snakes, always try to eat their prey head first.

How a Snake Eats

A garter snake has six rows of small, sharp, backward-curving teeth. These teeth hold the animal and get it in the right position for swallowing.

This isn't easy. Try eating a hot dog without using your hands. Pick it up with just your mouth and start to eat it. Don't let any bites fall out of your mouth, and don't set the hot dog down. Now, imagine a snake doing that with a kicking, slippery live frog.

When a garter snake grabs a small animal, it eats it as quickly as it can. But with a larger frog or mouse, the snake must use its jaws to get the animal head-first into its mouth. In this way, the arms and legs of the prey fold down and don't get stuck in the snake's throat.

Chapter 6

Hibernation and Reproduction

Garter snakes that live in cold regions hibernate during the winter months. Species living in Canada hibernate for more than half of the year. A snake hibernates in a den, a hole in the ground that lies under the frost. Here the snake is safe from freezing. Hundreds, sometimes thousands, of garter snakes may hibernate together in thick clumps.

This western terrestrial garter snake lives in Yellowstone National Park.

Mating Season

Most garter and ribbon snakes mate in the spring, after they crawl out of their winter dens. Males usually come out first from the den. When a female comes out, the male snakes get very excited.

Every male wants to be the one to mate with the female. There may be over 100 males trying to mate with a female. These giant groups of wiggling garter snakes are called mating balls. You can sometimes see them near a snake den.

Baby Snakes

Garter snakes are **ovo-viviparous**. That means the baby snakes grow inside of the female within clear egg sacks. The babies feed from an egg yolk, just like a baby chicken does.

As the young grow larger, they take up more and more space within the female. The mother snake has to stop eating as the babies continue to grow. She lives from her own fat while going as long as several weeks without food.

A baby snake emerges from the birth sac during the moment of birth.

The tiny baby garter snake is an easy prey for birds and small mammals.

By keeping the growing young within her, the female garter snake gives her babies a better chance to survive. In cold climates, she can keep the babies warmer. Also, the mother snake can protect her babies by hiding or fighting. Eggs that must hatch outside the mother have less protection from predators like foxes or raccoons.

Birth Day

Garter snakes give birth to live young in the late summer or early fall. A large common garter snake can give birth to as many as 85 young. Smaller species give birth to between four and 20 young. After birth, the young snake pushes its way out of its birth sac. The mother doesn't help and usually won't stay very long with her young.

After the birth, it is important for the female to eat large amounts of food before hibernation. If she doesn't eat enough, she may starve. A female breeds every two or three years. The rest of the time, she is eating to prepare for the next time she gives birth.

Chapter 7

Humans and the Garter Snake

Garter snakes live closer to people than any other species of snake. We find them in our backyards, in our city parks, beside roads, and near streams and creeks. Sometimes, garters use our house foundations for their hibernating dens.

Many people have caught garter snakes and kept them as pets. After they are handled for a short time, garter snakes become very tame. Unfortunately, many pet snakes die while in captivity.

Many people don't know what to feed garter snakes. Garters don't eat ants or dried turtle food. They can't eat food that's too large for them to swallow and digest. They must have a supply of water. And their cages must be warm enough to allow them to digest their food.

Snake Watching

The best way to study garter snakes is to find them in the wild. If you sneak up on a garter snake, you may be able to sit close by without scaring it. Then, you can watch the snake as it hunts or lies in the sun.

Some people want to get an even closer look. If you want to catch a garter snake, be sure to handle it gently. Look at its color and the scales on its back and belly. Notice how the scales differ around its lips and eyes. See if you can tell if it is a female or a male. Males have a long, slender tail that joins evenly with the body. Females have a thicker body and a thinner tail. In a female snake, you can easily see where the tail begins.

Don't handle a snake right after it has eaten. The snake may throw up its meal. Don't keep a snake overnight. And always return the snake to the same spot where you caught it.

Snakes are interesting animals to watch and learn about. Find out how many different species of snakes live in your area. See how many you can find. Try to take some pictures of the different snakes. Keep a record of your studies. Learning about snakes and their natural world can be fun and rewarding.

Glossary

albino–an animal lacking the color cells needed to have its natural color. An albino's eyes will be red, its hair white, and its skin a pale white or light yellow.

brilles–thin, clear scales covering a snake's eyes. Brilles are also known as spectacles.

caterpillar motion–a motion used by snakes, especially larger ones, to move in a straight line

concertina motion–a motion used by snakes in a confined area or on a slippery surface

diurnal–active during the day

ecdysis–the process of shedding the outer layer of skin

herpetologist–a scientist who studies reptiles

Jacobson's organs–special glands in a snake's mouth used to taste or smell different scents

keels–the ridges running down the middle of a snake's scales

musk–a foul-smelling, thick liquid used by some animals for defense

ovo-viviparous–a type of reproduction where the young develop inside an egg inside the mother and are born alive

scutes–the large, belly scales found on snakes. A snake will use its scutes to move in caterpillar motion.

serpentine motion–a motion used by snakes to move along rough surfaces or in swimming

species–a group of animals that look alike and can breed with each other

spectacles–the thin, clear scales covering a snake's eyes. Spectacles are also known as brilles.

To Learn More

Arnold, Caroline. *Snake.* New York: Morrow Jr. Books, 1991.

Gross, Ruth Below. *Snakes.* New York: Four Winds Press, 1990.

Lavies, Bianca. *A Gathering of Garter Snakes.* New York: Dutton, 1993.

Simon, Seymour. *Snakes.* New York: Harper Collins, 1992.

Smith, Roland. *Snakes in the Zoo.* Brookfield, CT: Millbrook Press, 1992.

Magazines

Reptiles and Amphibians
Reptiles

Some Useful Addresses

Sonora Desert Museum
2021 N. Kinney Rd.
Tucson, Arizona 85743

National Zoological Park
3001 Connecticut Ave. NW
Washington DC   20008

Clyde Peeling's Reptiland
Route 15
Allenwood, PA   17810

Toronto Zoo
361A Old Finch Avenue
Scarborough, Ontario   M1B 5K7

Dallas Zoo
621 E. Clarendon
Dallas, Texas   75203

Index